TALES FROM THE GREEK MYTHS

I Am the God Hermes

Kostas Poulos
Illustrated by Sofia Papadopoulou

Translated by Leo Kalovyrnas

metaichmio

1st edition April 2018

ORIGINAL TITLE Κώστας Πούλος,
Είμαι ο Ερμής, Μεταίχμιο 2017

TRANSLATED FROM THE GREEK LANGUAGE BY Leo Kalovyrnas
ILLUSTRATED BY Sofia Papadopoulou

ISBN 978-618-03-1451-9
AUXIL. COMPU. CODE 81451
C.E.P. 4324 C.P. 9744

© 2017 METAICHMIO Publications
and Kostas Poulos

Bookstores
1. 18 ASKLIPIOU STR., 106 80 ATHENS
TEL. +30 210 3647433, FAX: +30 211 3003562
Internet Site: www.metaixmio.gr
e-mail: metaixmio@metaixmio.gr

2. POLYCHOROS, 118 IPPOKRATOUS STR., 114 72 ATHENS
TEL. +30 210 3003580, FAX: +30 211 3003581

For Orpheus

K.P.

I am Hermes. I was born in a cave, high up on a mountain in Arcadia called Cyllene. It was early morning, I remember. I didn't cry, I didn't whimper. I didn't do any of the things that normal babies do. My mother Maia was really happy. Most mothers tend to think they've given birth to a tiny god, but mine was absolutely certain about it. She put me in my cradle to sleep, but I would have none of it! I was not going to spend the first day of my life inside some dark cave. So I sneaked out and what did I see? All kinds of plants and flowers everywhere, animals big and small under the trees, and colourful birds flying in the sky. High up the sun was shining and life was beautiful!

'I'm Hermes, and I'm a god!' I shouted.

My voice burst out of my mouth strong and loud and came back to me on the wind, as if taunting me, 'I'm Hermes, and I'm a gooood...'

I was so happy! I wanted to make the most of the first day of my life, but how?

A nightingale showed me how: by singing! At once I fashioned a lyre out of the shell of a tortoise and began to play music. The nightingale almost choked with envy.

and I'm a gooood...

I ran down the mountain all the way to the shores of the great Corinthian bay, which to me looked like a ditch full of salt water. I didn't hesitate at all. I leapt and landed on the far side without getting a single toe wet. Back in the cave, mother was fretting and looking for me everywhere.

'Hermes, where are you? Please come back home!' she shouted, for the cave was our home.

But I had already crossed half the country and reached the far north. It was there that I found what I had been looking for: Apollo's cattle. Apollo is my half-brother; we have a different mother, but share the same father: the god Zeus!

With no hesitation, I snatched about fifty of Apollo's cattle on the sly and took them faraway to Peloponnesus. But that's not all; I came up with a sneaky plan to confuse my brother: I made them walk backwards. Truth be told, what I did is called stealing, but I was too young to know. When thieves found out about what I'd done, they were thrilled, and so ever since they worship me as their god. I did try to come up with some excuse later on, but unfortunately you only need to steal once and then you're stuck with being branded as a thief forever. I ended up being called a cattle-raider and a robber god, and so all thieves and robbers that risk going to jail pray to me to save them.

Exhausted from my adventures on the first day of my life, I returned to the cave. It must have been around 8 in the evening, and my mother told me off for being out so late and then shooed me off to bed.

In the meantime, Apollo was searching for his missing cattle all over Greece, but he could not find them. He even came to our cave to look for them. I heard him come in and I pretended I was sleeping like a baby.

'Get yourself out of bed right now and tell me what you've done with my cattle!' Apollo shouted shaking my cradle.

A huge big quarrel ensued. In the end, we decided to go see our dad on Mount Olympus and have him settle our spat.

When Zeus found out what I'd done already on my first day alive, he burst into laughter. He was extremely pleased with me and felt very proud, but at the same time he didn't want to upset Apollo.

'Go on,' he ordered us, 'shake hands right this minute, you lot. Brothers shouldn't fight.' I immediately obeyed my dad's command, so I took out my lyre and began to play and sing.

Apollo, who happens to be the god of music, got a tad jealous of my playing. 'Give me the lyre and I'll give you all my cattle in return,' he said.

So that's how my brother and I became friends and all was well between us. Zeus kept me by his side on Mount Olympus. He made me his emissary and messenger. He gave me a winged staff, called kerykeion or caduceus, a winged cap, called petasos, and a pair of winged sandals, so that I could fly fast and deliver his commands. With just a simple lyre I had gained my place on Olympus. Everyone was impressed by the great bargain I had struck. When merchants got wind of this, they made me their god.

It was really nice on Olympus. From high above we could see all the cities and villages, and mortals milling about like tiny ants. They ploughed their fields or travelled to the four corners of the world in their ships. My father Zeus would send me on errands. I'd fly from one place to the next to deliver his messages to gods and mortals alike. In my spare time I studied and did a lot of research. That's how I discovered letters and numbers. Mortals found out about that too, so they made me god of letters as well. They knew that whoever believed in the god Hermes would be able to solve the hardest problems.

One day Zeus asked me to help him face Argus, a gigantic monster that had a hundred eyes!

No one could beat this monster because even when he slept, some of his eyes remained open, watching. But I was cunning! With my music I managed to lull him to sleep and make him close all hundred eyes – for all eternity. Ever since I'm known as the Argus slayer.

Another time, Zeus sent me to the island of Circe. Now Circe was a sorceress who had transformed Odysseus's shipmates into pigs. She was about to turn Odysseus into a pig too, but I got there in the nick of time and saved him. I flew like a seagull over the waves and gave him a magic herb that rendered the sorceress's spell useless. It was thanks to my help that Odysseus managed to return to his home in Ithaca in the end. Once there, he killed all the suitors

that were vying for his wife Penelope's hand in marriage and the throne. After they had died, it was my duty to transport them to the Underworld. They were all extremely upset and some of them sorely regretted antagonising Odysseus. They cried all the way to the Underworld, but there was nothing I could do for them, because death cannot be undone, not even by the gods.

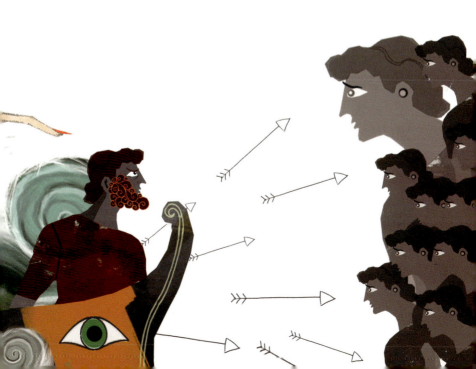

But what does a god look like? A lot of people have believed in me, yet no one had ever seen my face. It's hard to describe what I look like in words. Poets have tried, as have authors, and painters. But there is one artist who managed to capture me perfectly, the sculptor Praxiteles. One evening, I went to his place while he slept. The sculptor was overjoyed to see me. He thought he was dreaming.

'People must find out what I look like,' I told him. 'Only you can achieve this feat. Take this block of marble and start chiselling away at it carefully. Don't rush. You'll find me hiding inside. Release me, so that all mortals may admire me.'

And so he did. Praxiteles started chiselling the rock with great patience until I appeared from inside, I, Hermes. Now I stand tall and proud at the Olympia Museum. Lots of people come to see me and admire me. I look so life-like that people believe I am alive, and if anyone should ask me who I am, I'll shout, 'I'm Hermeees, and I'm a gooood!'

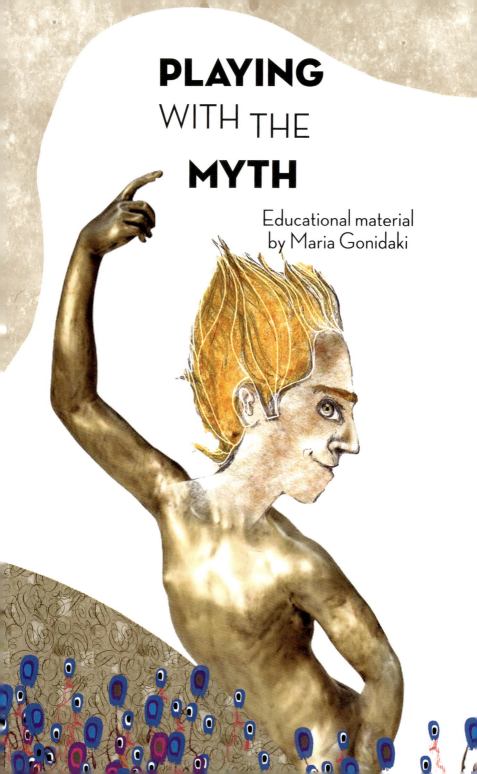

PLAYING WITH THE MYTH

Educational material
by Maria Gonidaki

LET'S LEARN ABOUT... THE GOD HERMES

The ancient Greeks worshipped dozens of gods and goddesses: not just the twelve Olympian deities but lots of other deities that were chiefly regional, which means that they were worshipped only in specific parts of the country. The most prominent ones in the religion of all ancient Greeks, however, were the twelve Olympians.

Hermes, one of the most beloved gods, was the son of Zeus and Maia, who was one of the daughters of Atlas, the giant who held up the sky on his shoulders for eternity.

Hermes was born in a cave on Mount Cyllene in Arcadia. The tiny god showed how clever and cunning he was on the very first day he was born. After fashioning the first lyre in the world from the shell of a tortoise and the entrails of a sheep for strings, he travelled to Pierria at the foot of Mount Olympus and managed to steal fifty cattle from his brother's herd. He came up with the sneaky idea to make them walk backwards all the way to Peloponissos, so that his brother, Apollo, would not be able to trace their hoofprints. But Apollo, being the god of divination, discovered who the thief was and got terribly angry. Luckily, thanks to Zeus's intervention, the two gods made peace. Hermes gave his lyre to Apollo as a gift, and Apollo gave his brother the cattle he had stolen, plus the caduceus, which is a golden staff, so that everyone would see that Hermes was the divine messenger carrying Zeus's commands.

Being the emissary of the gods, Hermes delivered their messages, and so Zeus entrusted him with the most important missions. However, in order for Hermes to deliver the messages properly, he had to be a true master of language. That is why he became known as the god of speech and eloquence. He was also considered to be the inventor of letters and numbers. According to a version of the myth, he was the one who invented fire, and the first lyre. He was the protector of merchants and travellers, but also of thieves. Another important job Hermes was tasked with was to guide the souls of the dead to Hades; that's why he was often called conductor of souls.

In other words, Hermes was the god that united three realms: the realm of the Olympian gods, the realm of mortals, and the world of the dead.

WORD GAME

▶ Fill in the missing words and you'll find the name of the mountain Hermes was born on.

1. The staff Hermes always carried with him.
2. Hermes invented the first …
3. Who taught Hermes how to sing?
4. While still an infant, Hermes stole the cattle of …
5. The only artist who managed to capture what Hermes looked like was called …
6. Hermes's grandfather was called …
7. Hermes was born in a …

1. C A D U C E U S
2. L Y R E
3. N I G H T I N G A L E
4. A P O L L O
5. P R A X I T E L E S
6. C R O N U S
7. C A V E

ANSWERS: 1. CADUCEUS, 2. LYRE, 3. NIGHTINGALE, 4. APOLLO, 5. PRAXITELES, 6. CRONUS, 7. CAVE

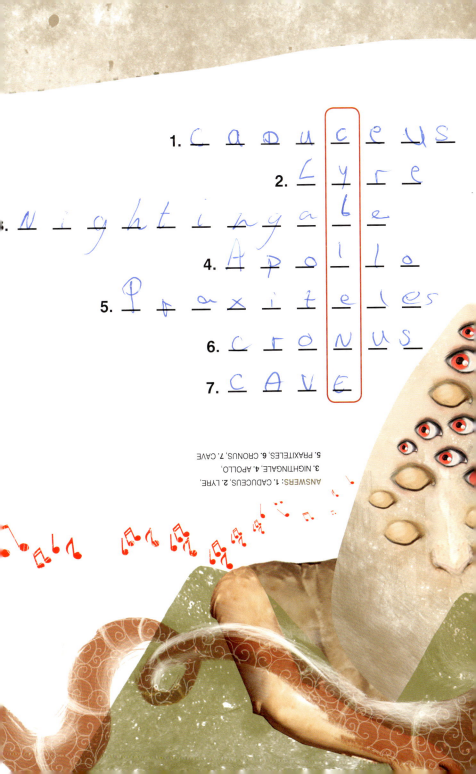

- In ancient Greek imagery, the god Hermes
  - wore the petasos, his winged cap;
  - held a caduceus, a golden staff with two intertwining snakes;
  - wore winged sandals or boots.

- Take a close look at the following images of Hermes from ancient Greek vases and circle the petasos, the caduceus, and the winged sandals.

Vatican Museum

- The marble statue in the photo below is Hermes by Praxiteles. This work of art was crafted in the 4th century BC and is considered to be the only original piece by that great artist surviving to this day.
- Note how Hermes is portrayed.
  - Does he seem calm or agitated? Does he look like the restless Hermes shown on the vases on the opposite page?
  - Are there any of his symbols present?

Olympia, Archaeological Museum

THINK ABOUT THIS...

This particular statue shows Hermes holding the infant Dionysus, who seems to be trying to grab something from Hermes's hand. Look up on the Internet or in an encyclopaedia the myth that tells how Dionysus was born.

▶ Hermes was known as a trickster god. All cultures have tales of the trickster, a crafty creature who uses cunning to get food, steal precious possessions, or simply cause mischief. Can you name any other gods, legendary figures or fictional characters that are also considered to be tricksters?

- In Norse mythology, he is a shape-shifting trickster god, who sometimes helps the gods and sometimes behaves in a malicious manner.

  — — — —

- A nature sprite in English folklore, also going by the name of Hobgoblin. He is famous for mischievous pranks and practical jokes, but can also prove helpful.

  — — — —

- A comic book supervillain who likes to hurt his enemies with tricks like explosive teddy bears.

  — — — — — — — — —

ANSWERS:
LOKI
PUCK
TRICKSTER

- The caduceus or kerykeion is the most prominent symbol of Hermes. In ancient depictions it looks like a staff on top of which two snakes form a circle, their heads jutting out like horns.

In newer depictions it is shown like a staff with two snakes intertwining, and two wings at the top, like in the drawing below.

Feel free to paint the caduceus in your favourite colours.

THINK ABOUT THIS TOO...

The caduceus was carried by ambassadors and orators, so it became a symbol of peace, abundance and wealth.

Sofia Papadopoulou

Sofia Papadopoulou lives and works in Athens, Greece. She studied Architecture at the National Technical University of Athens. After completing her studies, she began working professionally on children's book illustrations. She has worked with publishers such as Metaichmio, Kedros, Psichogios and Ocelotos. For the illustration of the book I'm telling you I'm not a monster, Kedros 2011, she was nominated for DIAVAZO magazine's awards. In January 2013 she exhibited her works as a solo artist in the 'Laspi Workshop' and has participated in various festivals. She was a student of the painter and sculptor Vasilis Katsivelakis, and is now being tutored by painter Pavlos Nikolakopoulos. Alongside her artistic work, she is a technical drawing instructor, preparing students for entering architectural and design faculties.

Kostas Poulos

Kostas Poulos was born in Elikonas, Viotia. He studied philology at the Universities of Athens, Würzburg, and Munich, and worked as a secondary school teacher both in Greece and abroad. He has written, translated and adapted several books for adults but chiefly for children for many publishing houses (Livanis, Boukoumanis, To Rodakio, Papadopoulos, Metaichmio). Some of his most famous books include: *Sun in the Garden*, *Half A Chocolate Is A Joke*, *One Ice-Cream Lasts Too Little*, *Nikos And The Wolf*, *Theofilos The Painter*, *Maria Callas*, *Scheherazade*, etc. His series of children's books The Greek Ones (Papadopoulos Publishers) includes classical texts of Greek literature from Homer to the present day especially adapted for kids. Poulos has also worked as a reader, editor, and reviewer for magazines and newspapers. His work has been translated into other languages and adapted for the theatre.

TALES FROM THE GREEK MYTHS
SERIES

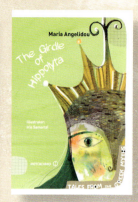
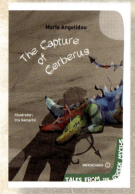
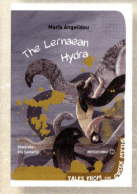
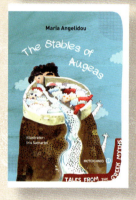

www.metaixmio.gr